SPIRIT GUIDES

Other Books by The Author

Invitation to Success:
Nobel Acton's Eleven Habits
of Creativity and Innovation
(Tenacity Press)

Follow Your Bliss, with Susan J. Sparrow
(Tenacity Press)
-Original Printings by Avon / Wm. Morrow-

Write From the Heart: Unleashing the
Power of Your Creativity
(Nataraj Publishing)

Zuni Fetishes: Using Native American
Objects for Meditation, Reflection & Insight
(HarperCollins & Book of the Month Club)

Mind Jogger: Intuitive Problem
Solving Companion
(Celestial Arts)

Lens Of Perception
(Celestial Arts/10 Speed Press)

Inner Guides Audio Cassette
(Tenacity Press)

The Well Body Book
(Bookworks-Random House)
-Out of Print-

SPIRIT GUIDES

By

Hal Zina Bennett, Ph.D.
With Susan J. Sparrow

TENACITY PRESS

ISBN 0-9656056-4-7
Printed by Morris Publishing
Cover design by Morris Publishing

10 9 8 7 6 5

Dedicated to
that quiet seeking spirit
within each of us,
constantly reaching
for a greater truth.

Acknowledgments

Upon the completion of a manuscript, we too often pack it up, send it off in the mail, and put it out of mind until the finished books turn up on our doorstep, or begin appearing in bookstores. However, no book would be possible without the efforts of a great many people behind the scenes: editors, graphic arts people, printers, people working in the offices that supervise the printing and shipping, book distributors, book sellers, and finally the readers. No book can hope to be successful without this vast collective of people who are involved in the process.

It is sad, I think, that authors rarely get to meet, or even learn the names of the many people who make it all possible. And when I begin to try to thank even the people I've come to know during the production of a book, I invariably leave someone out. So, without naming names, I want to extend my thanks to you all. Your work is deeply appreciated.

There are so many teachers who have helped to open my eyes a bit. I'm sure that many of my teachers would still tell you I have been a slow and stubborn student. There may be a couple who point to me with a certain degree of pride. There are those who didn't even know they were my teachers, who perhaps even believed us adversaries. I thank you all.

Like most people who teach, I do believe that our greatest teachers are our students. So, a special debt of gratitude goes out to all of you who have participated in our workshops over the years.

Most of all, I want to acknowledge my life partner and wife, Susan J. Sparrow. She has held a light for me all the years we have been together, reminding me of my path when I am off, loving me when I had forgotten how to love myself, and...last but not least, keeping the bills paid. She is my inspiration, my critic, and the love of my life.

Finally, no list of acknowledgments would be complete without mentioning our children, grand-children, parents, syblings, friends, cousins, inlaws and extended family members. Together we are all reminders of the larger whole in which we are all participants.~

-Hal Zina Bennett, Ukiah, California, June 1997

CONTENTS

Introduction

In the past few years I have received numerous requests for a compact book that would give easy to follow instructions for getting a spirit guide, and which would include stories about how I have used spirit guides in my own life. This turned out to be a larger challenge for me than I'd anticipated. I didn't want to be repetitive but if I were to tell the truth about how this practice developed for me, the only way I could do it with integrity was to retell material that I'd already published in previous books or essays. It required, in some cases, that I also tell more complete details about those events that had influenced me.

When I began asking people for their opinions about this, I met with some surprising responses. I found overwhelming support to put into one place those stories which authenticated breakthroughs in my own use of spirit guides, even though I had discussed these elsewhere. In fact, there was widespread agreement that no book I'd write on the subject would be complete without these anecdotes. People wanted a book that made the subject highly accessible and personal--simple, straight-forward and *real.* To the best of my ability, and with Susan's encouragement and support, I have followed the advice of my readers.

What you'll find in this book, along with easy to follow instructions for getting your own guides, are the stories of the three key turning points that made spirit guides so important for me. I have woven these together with new information about the importance of such guides in all our lives and why there is renewed interest in them now.

Ancient Wisdom in the Electronic Age

Our interest in spirit guides is perhaps as old as humanity itself. Throughout recorded history, and on virtually every continent, we find examples of how people have worked with these guides. Primarily, they have always given us access to the spiritual and *imaginal* realms. They have helped us shift our perceptions from the world of our senses to the "invisible reality" of emotion and spirit.

Today there are business people, scientists, artists,

teachers, salespeople, doctors, college professors, psychotherapists, scientists and health professionals who turn to their spirit guides for assistance on a regular basis. Many people learning how to use inner guides for the first time have remarked that after learning about them, they realized they had been accessing this source of knowledge unconsciously most of their lives. In most instances, they had just done it automatically, without an awareness of how to do it at will. After learning about spirit guides, however, they are able to access their spirit guides by choice rather than only serendipitously.

One of the insights we get after learning about spirit guides is that the boundaries of the self extend far beyond our immediate environment. We begin to experience new perceptions of the self. We see that we are spiritually linked with people halfway around the world, and with those who lived hundreds of years ago. We begin to see that we emerge from and are part of a single consciousness that is limited by neither time nor space. We are just as affected by events in the distant past as we are by those in the immediate present. And our spirit guides can even give us partial access to the future.

For most of us, insights provided by spirit guides can seem quite distant from our daily lives, where most of our attention is focused on events right in front of us. Yet, psychologists and spiritual teachers warn us that unless we do get in touch with the spiritual and psychological truths that profoundly influence our lives, we are not free to make truly informed and viable choices.

Throughout Western society we are undergoing a major shift in our understanding of the self. We begin to see that the human body is not merely a mass of protoplasm whose movements are run by the brain but is, rather, an energy being, a center of vibrancy, whose waves radiate out beyond the immediate environment through time and space. Moreover, these waves respond to and interact with an infinite variety of other waves.

We are coming to see that our human forms are singular manifestations of a larger energy being--call it Universal Light, the Life Force, God, or whatever other term you wish to apply--and that we in fact exist within a body of energy that extends infinitely throughout our own planet and out into the vast, unlimited universe. The energy of which we are a part transcends space and time, connecting us all, regardless of where or even when we have lived.

Jesuit paleontologist Teilhard de Chardin, described a "thinking layer"--or *noosphere*--that envelopes the Earth. This layer is activated, in part, by each and every conscious being. In effect, we are each like one cell in a giant brain, contributing to a whole that is too large for any of us to fully comprehend, Teilhard says:

> This noosphere is just as extensive and coherent as any other sphere of our planet, be it the atmosphere, the lithosphere, the hydrosphere, or the biosphere. Outside and above the biosphere, the noosphere constitutes the thinking layer, which, since its germination at the end of the Tertiary period, has spread over and above the world of plants and animals.

As we become increasingly familiar with the use of spirit guides, we connect with more and more of this thinking layer, or noosphere, of our planet. And we begin to understand our part in it, the implied responsibility of participating in life at that level, and that we, in turn, receive much in return for opening ourselves more fully to it. We see that we are no more separated from the Earth's noosphere than are our brain cells separated from our brains. Individual consciousness seamlessly merges with and emanates from the noosphere.

There's a wonderful quote of Lewis Thomas' that describes this relationship very well:

> We still argue the details, but it is conceded almost everywhere that we are not the masters of nature

that we thought ourselves; we are as dependent on the rest of life as are the leaves or midges or fish. We are part of the system. One way to put it is that the Earth is a loosely formed, spherical organism, with all its working parts linking in symbiosis.

It is my belief that only by gaining greater knowledge about, and skill with, the contents of our inner worlds, can we solve the chief problem of today--whether or not we will destroy our planet, render it uninhabitable by life as we know it, or fully embrace it and help it flourish, so that it may support and enjoy our future generations. We have the technology to go either way. But the choice about how to use that power may or may not be a *rational* one. Our inner worlds often work in mysterious ways, and we must learn to accept and apply the wisdom we are offered in this way. Otherwise, we are destined to repeat the errors of the past.

The more familiar we become with our inner worlds, and the more we honor our connectedness with the noosphere, the more we are likely to protect and love that which nurtures us, the Earth herself. And the more connected we feel with the cosmos, the more we will receive the bounties of Mother Earth and the spirit of life that is the special gift of this wondrous planet.

The more you explore the world of spirit guides, the more you'll discover a certain familiarity about the territory they inhabit. In fact, as this familiarity grows your visits to this place within your consciousness will be like coming home.

Through our use of spirit guides we come to know new levels of comfort within ourselves, along with a growing appreciation for our spiritual nature. Spirit guides are literally spiritual companions and counselors who can communicate with us in simple, direct ways, tapping the wisdom of the noosphere.

The wealth of knowledge we find through spirit guides can be applied in any number of ways--in developing richer personal relationships, in improving emotional and physical wellbeing, in having an increased ability to face problems and find solutions in everyday life, in creative endeavors, and in tapping into the powers of what some people call the *sixth sense*, that is, the intuitive or psychic side of our beings, that connects us with the greater whole.

Carl Jung, recognized as one of the modern world's foremost leaders in the exploration of human consciousness, once called this inner world "the greatest of all cosmic wonders."

Spirit guides are a very normal and natural part of the human experience. As you gain more practice with them, you will probably discover, as thousands of others have, that the experience is not new to you. You may recall that, as a very young child, you had an imaginary playmate. Or perhaps you had a favorite doll you talked with, seeking counsel and comfort when parents or playmates hurt your feelings. As you grew older, you adopted heroes--movie stars, rock stars, artists, characters from fiction, or even the memory of a favorite relative--who also served this purpose. In quiet times, feeling the need for their strength, their company, or their counsel, you allowed yourself to daydream, to inwardly converse with these people of the inner landscape.

The mystery about the source of spirit guides remains, but we do know that there are many records of conversations with such beings, most of them highly beneficial, which appear in literature, psychology, philosophy, music, science, and religious texts throughout the world. In the final analysis it does not matter what the inner guides really are--where they come from, or what they represent in the world. Millions of people, throughout the ages, have found them to be the source of knowledge, comfort and revelation that clearly improve the quality of life.

However you choose to use your guides, bear in mind that just as in any other personal relationship in your life, you are responsible for choosing to accept or reject the information they provide. There is a wonderful story told by Sun Bear, who brought us so many valuable teachings from the Native American traditions. He tells how he had a spirit guide who was the reincarnation of a great warrior, who'd lived centuries before. Sun Bear had great respect for this guide but each time he followed the spirit guide's advice Sun Bear got into trouble. Bewildered by this, Sun Bear went to his own teacher and told him what was happening. His teacher, a wise old medicine man, listened to Sun Bear's story with interest. When the story was done the old man turned to his student and said, simply, "Dead don't make you wise!"

The moral of this story is obvious: Spirit guides, like any other persons in our lives, are not infallible. Get to know your guides by contacting and communicating with them on a regular basis for a month or two before you start following their advice and counsel. The most enlightened of them will not prescribe a path for you, any more than the most enlightened counselor in our outer lives would do. The most valuable information they provide will come through as flashes of insight or gentle suggestions that will help you make subtle changes in the way you view your own life. Always keep Sun Bear's advice in mind, that being in the form of a spirit doesn't automatically make your counselor infallible.

With these considerations in mind, go forward on your journey to the world of spirit guides with a sense of adventure, exploration and play. Probe the mysteries of this realm with healthy skepticism but allow your heart and your mind to stay open to the many benefits it offers. Just as in our daily lives in the physical world, we are most open to both the joys and the special moments of profundity when we remember to bring along the best of our own humor and humility. These are required equipment for any spiritual seeker since they remind us that in our present lives, as physical beings, our egos as well as our five senses will mask over what we can know of the universe. Just as the Bible tells us, within our human limitations we can only "see through a glass darkly."

Spirit guides provide glimpses beyond the truths of the physical realm. But at best they can only point to tiny windows that give us a view of the infinite reality beyond. Still, what our spirit guides offer is worth celebrating, for they can provide piercing insights that confirm our spiritual identity.~

The Nature of Spirit Guides

"Thoughts are like animals in the forest, or people in a room, or birds in the air... If you should see people in a room, you would not think that you had made those people, or that you were responsible for them..."
--C.G. Jung, attributed to
his spirit guide Philemon

S cience teaches that we ourselves generate our thoughts, our fantasies, our dreams and even our moments of epiphany. Growing up in the scientific tradition, as most of us have, we are tempted to dismiss talk about spirit guides or guardian angels, which belong to that imaginary realm, as wistful thinking, if not sheer madness. Yet, there are those like C.G.Jung, one of the most highly celebrated psychologists of the past two centuries--note the quote I have included above--who thoroughly believed that such entities were real and that they represented a source of wisdom beyond our

1

direct experience.

To clarify, the above quote was part of Philemon's (spirit guide) explanation when Jung asked him to explain what he was. Philemon essentially told him two things--that thoughts had lives of their own and were not merely a person's creation, and that spirit guides such as Philemon, also had identities separate from the brain of the person they served.

Most of us have had at least some experience with these entities we call spirit guides. Maybe there was a moment when we thought we heard an inner voice advising us about something we were about to do. Or in a somnolent, dreamy moment we had the impression that someone was nearby comforting us when we were blue or encouraging us to go forward when we were stalled with self-doubt. While we might have had such experiences in childhood, and perhaps even in adulthood, the encounter was fleeting. Try as we might, we can't seem to call these kinds of experiences into our consciousness at will. At best, they appear serendipitously, then slip away the moment we realize what's happened.

When I was a small boy growing up in Michigan, I had an imaginary friend I called Alex. He was like a trusted older brother, eight or ten years my senior, and infinitely wiser than I in the ways of the world. When Alex was with me, we talked. Walking down the street in the suburban neighborhood where I lived, we carried on lengthy inner dialogues, and to me Alex was as real as any other person in my life.

My parents were at least tolerant when I told them about Alex though I am certain that had they understood how important he was in my daily life they might have been more concerned. Where I grew up, the idea of "talking to yourself" was not considered to be healthy behavior, to put it mildly. My parents' reaction, at worst, was to indulge me, treating my stories about my imaginary friend as "cute make-believes" that I would eventually outgrow.

I don't believe that my experience is unique. Over the years, I've taught thousands of people about the use of spirit guides. Time and time again, I hear stories similar to mine, where the childhood contacts with these guides were profound, yet were discouraged by wellmeaning adults or by older children. It is for this reason that I relate my own experiences, to assure readers that what they may have encountered in their own early lives around these guides was not unique.

If my parents indulged me in my *imaginary friendship* with Alex, my peers were less than kind. After suffering through the jibes of my playmates about "the little man who wasn't there," I found that I was better off not mentioning him at all. I kept him to myself. He comforted me when I was afraid. And even when I was six or seven years old he began tutoring me in ideas that no other older person in my life had ever discussed. He was the first to point out to me that the physical world in which we live is not at all what it appears to be, that there was a much greater reality beyond this one, indeed responsible for this one, that I would one day come to see more clearly. He taught me to contemplate the infinite, instructing me to gaze at the stars in the evening sky and ponder the mysteries. When pets in the neighborhood had babies, or when human mothers did, he focused my attention on the miracle of the life spirit that animated these new beings. Every new birth was a reminder that there was a power far greater than any human being, greater even than Nature herself. And everything I experienced, even my own thoughts, was an expression of this power.

Alex did not teach with words except to instruct me where and how to look. To look beyond the stars into infinite space. To look upon physical existence as a curtain, behind which was a larger truth. To look beyond the corporeal reality of a newborn, miraculous though this might be, to catch a glimpse of the Source that animated it. Alex' gentle coaching was the only metaphysical instruction I ever got in my childhood. Indeed, I was in my mid-twenties before I discovered that there were regular people who discussed such matters!

Gradually, as the pressures of my peers increased, I pushed my thoughts of Alex to the back of my mind, knowing it was somehow not acceptable. As I did so, Alex' presence in my life, at least on a conscious level, diminished. In fact, like a friend rebuffed he pretty much disappeared from my life.

It was not until I was in my twenties, when I was introduced to the writings of C.G. Jung, that I renewed my interest in spirit guides. Jung's work gave at least a hint of support and confirmation for my experiences with these elusive entities. Even so, I did not immediately let beings such as Alex back into my life. Jung spoke of the <u>anima</u> and <u>animus</u>, figures that appear in our unconscious, and which seem to us to be autonomous, that is, spirit beings whose personalities are separate from our own.

Jung said that his theories about the anima and animus were "not a question of anything *metaphysical*." Yet, he admitted that the spirits or inner guides could be "as rich and strange as the world itself," and that as we begin "making them conscious we convert them into bridges to the un-conscious." For Jung, the anima and animus represented male and female functions or personal characteristics that, for highly individualized reasons, were important to the person's overall vision of life. He claimed that these spirits and their functions had been noted by people in "primitive" societies for centuries.

It is interesting to note here that a few years later, while reading the work of the Northern Cheyenne philosopher and medicine man, Hyemeyohsts Storm, I would come upon these words: "Within every man there is the Reflection of a Woman, and within every woman there is the Reflection of a Man. Within every man and woman there is also the Reflection of an Old Man, an Old Woman, a Little Boy, and a Little Girl." Here, in the cosmologies of the Native American shaman, was further validation for spirit beings who communicated to us, and made their presence known to us through our consciousness. While Storm's insights intrigued me, I was primarily interested in western psychology at the time, and sought answers in Jung.

Jung taught me that as important as the functions or characteristics associated with the anima might be to us, we could not, or had not yet allowed ourselves to incorporate them into our personalities. So, at least on one level, these beings were manifestations, or off-shoots, of our own psychology. An anima might embody characteristics that we considered distasteful, and which we could not accept as part of our own personality. Or we might reject it for what others might view as positive reasons; for example, an anima might embody a sense of self-power that we could not imagine ourselves possessing because to do so would mean that we would have to give up the security of a dependency on a parent or other loved one. In order to have these characteristics in our lives without fully "owning" them, we invented these spirits of the unconscious so that we could have some of the benefits of these characteristics without fully incorporating them into our personality.

To maintain our separateness from these characteristics and, at the same time, experience a sense of completeness in our outer world, Jung postulated, we might seek relationships with real people who matched, or as closely as possible matched the anima that lived within our unconscious. However, there were dangers in seeking the real world *double* of these spirits; people in the outer world could never quite fill the bill. They would be mere *standins* who would leave us frustrated and bewildered. In addition, therapeutic work with people who attempted to do this, Jung found, revealed that the anima might defend its territory like a jealous lover or an overprotective parent, acting hurt or angry whenever we approached a person in the real world who might replace them. In that case, our emotional involvement with the anima or animus might result in our rejecting those persons in the outer world who threatened to replace the *inner guide*.

Jung believed that we could transform these guides

from being sources of conflict in our lives to becoming real helpers. And one did that by speaking to the animus, and asking it questions such as why it was present in our life. For example, Allen, a friend of mine who went through Jungian analysis, reported having difficulty maintaining lasting relationships with the women in his life. He desperately wanted a stable relationship but any time he got close to a woman he liked he began acting in an offensive "chauvinistic" manner that literally drove her away. Though he intellectually understood what he was doing, and did not like himself when he was being chauvinistic, he could do nothing to stop himself.

In the course of his work with the Jungian therapist, Allen discovered that he had an inner guide who was a middle aged woman called Alice. Alice embodied all the human values that he had been taught were "feminine." Though he felt a need for these feminine qualities in his life, he was unable to allow himself to consider them as elements of his own personality because, according to his father's values, this would have made him a "sissy."

Allen eventually discovered that Alice was jealous of his relationships with the real women in his life, and it had been as a result of protecting Alice that he had manifest the chauvinistic behavior that drove away his prospective lovers.

Eventually, Allen started talking directly with Alice, treating her as if she was an actual person in his life. He told her that she must stop interfering with other relationships in his life. He went through a period of feeling guilty for doing this. But he realized that as an adult he had every right to determine who and what entered his consciousness. Soon after this, Allen did establish a successful relationship with a woman, and was eventually happily married.

Following his laying the law down to Alice, this anima eventually adopted a helpful role in Allen's life. He turned to her whenever he wanted guidance in emotional matters. It was, after all, the woman's job to take care of such matters- -or so he had been led to believe by his parents. In time, Alice was transformed from being a source of conflict in his emotional relations to being a real helper.

One rather interesting aside is that after he was married, Allen became interested in cooking, and it soon became a deeply satisfying creative outlet--though it had been assigned to the woman's world in his father's eyes. When he was cooking, Allen said, he always had a strong sense of Alice's presence, as though she was helping him and fulfilling her own enjoyment of the culinary arts through him.

Beyond Anima and Animus

Jung as well as other psychologists have noted that there are other entities that can appear in our consciousness like the anima or animus but which are not products of our ego or personality. These may appear spontaneously in dreams, or through the use of *active imagination* (guided imagery or visualization), but in no way do their histories appear to be related to our own emotional struggles. In fact, they appear to be quite separate from the person perceiving them. For example, "channeled" entities such as Seth, made popular by the books of Jane Roberts, appear to be quite outside the everyday realms of the person receiving their words, would have to be viewed as something other than anima/animus.

It was in his memoirs that Jung described a conversation he had with his own spirit guide, Philemon, who was this latter kind of being. It is from his own comments that I drew the epigram for this chapter. I quote this in its entirety now:

I observed clearly that it was he (Philemon) who spoke, not I. He said I treated thoughts as though I generated them myself, but in his view thoughts were like animals in the forest, or people in a room, or birds in the air, and added, 'If you should see people in a room, you would not think that you

10

had made those people, or that you were responsible for them.' It was he who taught me psychic objectivity, the reality of the psyche... He confronted me in an objective manner, and I understood that there is something in me which can say things that I do not know and do not intend...

Upon reading this passage, and others concerning spirit guides in Jung's life, conflicts I had about my own childhood guide began to diminish. And I had a whole new set of questions to ask Alex, my tutor in the metaphysical realm.

Inner Guides As Teachers

As I began following Jung's model, I found that my task with at least some of the inner guides I encountered became one of accepting their importance in my inner life, and then allowing myself to learn from them, setting up the same kinds of sometimes skeptical, sometimes fully trusting relationships that I had with people in my outer world. And I found, indeed, that as I grew to know them, to recognize and accept their *human* strengths and weaknesses, my own personality took on their functions, just as it had done for the man in the above example. I could own the functions of character they represented.

In the 1970's I happened upon the research of Elmer and Alyce Green, published in their book *Beyond Biofeedback*. Their bio-feedback research, through the Menninger Foundation, made it clear that: "the unconscious mind did not distinguish between an imagined and a real experience." That which was imagined could have as dramatic affects on the body and the conscious mind as that which was experienced in the *real world through the senses.*

What bearing did this discovery have on inner guides? For me it was a great revelation; it suggested to me that in the final analysis it did not matter what the inner guides really were. The unconscious mind, which psychologists and neurophysiologists agree is the dominant force in our lives, experiences these persona just as it does any other "people" in our lives.

Given their potential affects on us, the first question that came to my mind was this: "How can I recognize an anima, or for that matter a spirit guide, who may be misadvising me, or giving me wrong information, in order to protect her own interests?" How could I determine who could be trusted and who couldn't in this inner world? I concluded that whether they were real or imagined, each one of us has a responsibility to weigh the value of whatever these beings bring to our lives. Sometimes they are right, sometimes wrong. Sometimes they were kind, sometimes cruel.

Whether they are real or not, one has to treat them as being, after all, "only human," just as capable of vanity and folly and error as the rest of us. But I would have to live through many adventures, and a few misadventures, before I'd begin to understand how to make use of spirit guides, that there would be a particular path I would find that would carry me through this metaphysical wilderness.

Learning To Live Outside the Boundaries

In the 1960s, I was, like many others of my generation, experimenting with mind-altering drugs. During a long stay in Mexico I took mescalin, in the form of *magic mushrooms*, with a person I would now call a shaman, though I did not know that name at the time. An entirely new vision of life opened up to me, one I did not understand, and since the shaman and I had no common language--he being an Indian, me being a *gringo* from north of the border--I could not get answered the myriad of questions pouring through my mind.

When I returned to the states, I continued to pursue this new vision of my life, and began taking peyote and LSD with another shaman I met, this time a man of Cherokee and Irish descent who I met in

California.

Thanks to peyote, I began to see how my inner world colored and gave shape to my outer world, just as Alex had taught. With my shaman-teacher, the elusive world of inner consciousness became increasingly tangible and viable. Indeed, during long hallucinatory episodes, I saw and spoke with people who had previously appeared only in my inner world. Now these people took on separate identities, including what appeared to be real physical bodies in the external world. It was as though I had projected mental holograms from my inner world to the outer one. Yet, these people clearly were separate from me. When they spoke I knew their words had not come from my own mind; like Alex, the spirit guide of my childhood, they said and did things that I could not predict.

At first puzzled and frightened by these apparitions who now seemed so real to me, my shaman friend explained that they were spirit guides, beings from my inner world, and that they were in fact autonomous, real and separate from me. He encouraged me to speak with them, which I did. As I spoke with them, sometimes aloud, sometimes only inwardly, I recognized that they had always been a part of me, that they had lived in my consciousness, appearing in my dreams and daydreams, for as long as I could remember. I saw that they had existences as real to me, and as separate as those of my friends and acquaintences in the physical world. Granted, there was a difference between the two worlds, that is, the physical and the ethereal, but one was no less real than the other. I saw that the inner world figures had a lot to do with how I operated in the world; my interests, fears, likes and dislikes all related to my relationships with them. In fact, this was the first time I began to understand how my success in life was often more profoundly affected by the inner world reality than by the outer one.

When the peyote wore off, some twenty hours later, I discussed what I had experienced with my shaman friend. He smiled and nodded, his face placid and maybe a little bemused, as though all my new insights were common knowledge--which to him they were. I wanted explanations. If he had any, he wasn't interested in giving them. In the end he just looked me in the eye and said, "That's right."

Annoyed by his glibness, I probed further. What was right? Was this the way everyone's inner world worked? "There is no inner and outer. It is all the same thing," he replied irritably. "Learn to see this." The subject was closed. The next thing I knew we were climbing into his car and driving across town to have breakfast at a "Denny's" restaurant near the freeway onramp.

Reflecting on the peyote experiences and my conversations with the spirit guides and other people who lived in my consciousness, it seemed to me that my spirit guides were emissaries between inner and outer worlds.

Over the next two or three years, I took peyote perhaps a dozen or more times. Thanks to the hallucinogens, I could carry on long conversations with the entities of my inner world, and even question what purpose this or that inner guide served in my life. On one occasion I even had a showdown with a character who had played tricks on me and manipulated me over the past years. Even while all this was occuring, I knew the difference between these ethereal manifestations and the "real" people in my life. At no time was I fearful that my communications with these entities were in any way pathological. This work seemed as natural and meaningful as anything I could imagine doing. Rather than fear or bewilderment, I finally experienced a great sense of relief, a feeling of "Aha! At last all the cards are on the table!"

To get to that point that I could consult with my inner guides without the stigma attached to this process during my childhood, I had to constantly struggle with my own doubts. Like so many people who had spirit guides, or "imaginary playmates," early in their lives, I had to overcome those early memories of humiliation and even parental concern. There's no doubt in my mind that what helped me move beyond this was a series of events that occurred around the time of my father's death, in 1973. It was at this time that I learned how the guides can help us in very direct and purposeful ways, giving us strength and knowledge to deal with some of life's greatest challenges.

Note: While I learned much from the peyote shaman with whom I worked, I do not advocate the use of this or any other psychotropic plant or substance without expert guidance by a person such as a shaman or psychotherapist who is trustworthy and experienced in the use of these powerful substances for spiritual revelation and growth.

Spirit Guides

A Glimpse of the Greater Reality

What is this greater reality? It views the mind as
more than a brain compiling information like a mere
computer. It views human consciousness as part of a
greater reality in (and perhaps beyond) time and space,
not as the epiphenomenon of an organism with a
limited time span in the physical body.
—Brian O'Leary, Ph.D.,
Exploring Inner and Outer Space

Undoubtedly one of the most dramatic uses of spirit guides, and one that confirmed my belief that they could be useful even at a practical level, came for me upon hearing that my father was dying. Dad was nearly 80 years old at the time and had lived a full and satisfying life. I am sure he was better prepared for his death than I or any of our other family members were.

19

I had no idea how to deal with his death. I got the news of his hospitalization over the phone, from 3,000 miles away, and immediately after that call I went to my office to make arrangements to fly back to Michigan to be with him in his last hours. As I sat in my study at home, I remembered that I had written down a dream I'd had of his death nearly two years before. Having done dream work for several years, I had a great number of journals to go through, but I was finally able to find the dream of my father's death and study what it said.

In the dream my father was lying in a hospital room. It was winter. There were two windows, one pointing east, one pointing north, and looking to the east I saw a huge harbor. There was a door leading from the north wall of this building down some wooden steps to a row of docks. In the dream my father died and I saw his spirit leave his body. I then led his spirit--which still had the shape of his body--to a strange looking boat, whose pilot, a man dressed like a fisherman and approximately my father's age, stood on the deck waiting for him.

My father and the boatman greeted each other in a friendly way, Dad a bit nervous, but not frightened. He seemed to be anticipating the meeting with a certain amount of excitement. The boatman and he shook hands, and then the two of them admired the boat, which had beautifully finished teak decks. My father, having been a furniture maker, had an eye for fine finishes and he was quite impressed with the workmanship of this boat.

At last the boatman told my father that it was time to go. Dad turned to me and to my surprise asked my permission to leave, which I gave him. He then went over a checklist he'd made up concerning each family member, asking me to confirm that they were all doing okay. It seemed that he did not feel good about leaving before he received this confirmation. I reassured him everyone was doing well, and I was certain they all gave him permission to leave us. He then asked me to say goodbye to them for him, and I promised him that I would. Then he and I embraced, kissed, and he got into the boat. The dream ended with my standing on the dock watching the boat disappear out over the horizon.

I read the dream and wept. At this time in my life I had tentatively begun communicating with Alex again. Surprisingly, I found that he had aged. He was no longer the teenaged boy I remembered from my childhood but was now a man approaching middle age. I had no sooner turned my thoughts to Alex than he instantly appeared in my mind's eye. When I told him about my father dying he said very quietly that I should go and be with him, and that I was to be his guide to the other side. I was appalled by the suggestion. I argued with Alex that I knew nothing

21

about such things, that I had never been with anyone dying and wouldn't know how to handle it.

Alex told me not to worry, that it would be difficult but that I would get help along the way and the whole thing would go quite smoothly.

"Exactly how will I get this help?" I asked.

"Oh, you know," he said, "you meet somebody and you ask."

He said this in a flippant manner, implying that this was so obvious and elementary that I should never have asked. I nevertheless pressed him to give me a sign, to tell me what I should be seeking in my helpers.

At this point he began to poke fun at me. He hunched up his shoulders, screwed up his face and in a rather humorous way, as if satirizing himself, he spoke in a voice reminiscent of Bela Lagosi playing Dracula. He said, "*Zee first person you meet will be an older voman. Go with her and she vill tell you very important information!*"

I did not like his clowning at all. I was quite put off by it, thinking it in poor taste to be making jokes about such a serious situation. His only response was to shrug off my criticism, as if to say, *have it your way. It makes no difference to me.*

A hour or so later I went down to the travel agency to pick up my plane ticket for the trip back to Michigan. On the way out I literally bumped into an older woman. I excused myself and backed away from her, with the intention of moving on. Then I recognized her as the real estate saleswoman from whom I'd purchased our house several years before.

"Ah, Hal Bennett," she said, "Are you taking a trip?"

I instantly noted that she spoke with a thick, southern Italian accent. Stunned, I remembered the accent Alex had assumed when he told me I would meet an *older woman* who would assist me. This was too much of a coincidence! Was it possible that Alex really had known this woman would appear?

Somewhat shakily, I told the woman that my father was dying and I was going back to Michigan to be with him.

"Ah hah, yes!" she said. "You must come to my office right now. I have something very important to tell you."

"Right," I replied, without a moment's hesitation, recalling my spirit guide's earlier admonishment.

Her office was only a few doors from the travel agency, and we went there immediately. She locked the outer door and invited me to sit down beside her desk. Then, like a teacher instructing a pupil she told me how less than a year before she had sat with her father as he was dying. It turned out he died from exactly the same disease that my father had. Without my asking her a single question, she gave me a huge amount of information about the disease and what would happen, how he would become extremely agitated and restless, how he would hallucinate, and how I might comfort him. She also said that for her the experience of sitting with her father in his death had been a "great privilege," as "wondrous as the birth of her children," and that even though she deeply mourned his loss, being present with him in his death had enriched her life.

"This is a great gift to you," she said. "You must open your heart and your mind to it completely."

I told her how grateful I was for her help. We hugged, and I promised that I'd report back to her as soon as I returned from my trip.

On the airplane to Detroit I thanked Alex for

encouraging me to listen to the older woman, to trust that the kind of help I needed would come. Alex told me to have faith that I would continue to get whatever assistance I required, and to look upon the dream I'd had as a guiding dream, a map for what I must do.

My brothers met me at the airport in Detroit, and that evening I went to the hospital. The man I saw in the bed bore only a vague resemblance to the mental image that I had of my father. His lips were parched and bleeding, and he was badly dehydrated despite an i.v. feeding fluids into his failing body.

Dad was happy to see me. He asked about my trip from California, and asked about his grandchildren. We made smalltalk, and from time to time he dozed off. In the beginning he was peaceful and outgoing, though his strength was obviously failing. But as that day passed, then another and another, his mood changed. He became agitated and impatient with the medical staff, didn't want them in his room. He asked to have the i.v. removed from his arm, which I did for him, and then he began refusing any further medication. In the last couple days of his life no-one but family members entered his room. We dismissed the medical staff and they happily made themselves scarce. It was clear that they did not like dealing with death.

As he severed himself more and more from the medical support system, Dad's dependence on us grew. I seemed able to calm him when he panicked, when he thrashed about on the bed, complaining of pain or his loss of self-control. It was Alex who helped me at these moments, explaining that all I needed to do was to place my hand lightly over my father's heart and stay in a peaceful place in my own mind by meditating. My father's body was no longer important; I had to address my attention to his spirit. This I did, and I was amazed at how well it went, calming him even more effectively than the hospital's pain drugs had done before he refused to take them any more.

Toward the second or third day he had begun hallucinating heavily, just as my friend the real estate woman had told me he would. The contents of these hallucinations were very meaningful, and very private.

When I sought Alex' help with Dad's hallucinations, he told me, "Let your father have these illusions. Do whatever you can to confirm his reality, whatever that reality might be to him. The hallucinations are his only reality at this moment. Don't argue with him or try to convince him they aren't real, because to him they are real. If he seems frightened about them, ask him what you can do to help, and then do it, though it may require you to take action in a world that you cannot see. Just keep in mind that there are many realities that cannot be confirmed by our five senses, and that is where you can be of the greatest service to your father now."

Following these instructions I spent a good part of one day and most of another miming out little rituals such as straightening up a bookshelf that wasn't there, or scratching the toes of my father's left leg which had been amputated many years before. Some of these rituals were on the order of daily housekeeping, some went much deeper than that, communicating with people whose presence I could not see but who were playing out important dramas in Dad's life.

One of the most disturbing things to me was a recurring image when I sat beside my father with my hand on his heart. He would grow peaceful, almost blissful. Then an image would come into my mind of him and me in an invisible vehicle of some sort, racing out over a desert. My father appeared to be enjoying this--but I wasn't. The speed picked up, and the faster we went the more nervous I became. Finally, I would jump, startled, and at that point I would leave my meditative space and my father would become increasingly agitated.

This experience happened several times. One afternoon my younger brother Paul came to relieve me, and I drove back to my mother's house to rest. On the way back I asked Alex what the ride in the invisible vehicle represented. He told me that it was Dad's image of his passage from life to death, and I had nothing to fear from it. I asked if this meant that my dream about the passage taking place in a boat had been wrong. Alex said no, it was not wrong, but everyone had his own image to symbolize his passage, and the boat was mine. The passage would be the same, he said, regardless of the vehicle involved.

I asked Alex what I should do about the startle reflex because I did not want to continue projecting my own fear to my father. Alex instructed me that I should go for a walk to a specific place I had often gone as a teenager. I was told exactly where to go, which was a cedar swamp at the edge of the lake where I'd grown up.

It was in the dead of winter, and I had to borrow hiking boots and warm clothes to get where I was going. Directed by Alex, I came to a clearing in the woods. There before me was a primitive structure I'd made as a child. I had cut and lashed together several saplings, forming a crude pyramid frame with a fallen tree at the center, upon which I'd often sat. As a teenager, I'd intended to build a little hut in this spot. I'd planned that the lashed-together saplings would be the framework for the roof. When I built them, twenty years before, I had no idea that they'd formed a pyramid.

Sitting within the pyramid, I turned toward the lake, closed my eyes, and began to meditate. A few minutes passed. Then I imagined that I saw a figure in a red hunting coat coming toward me. I sensed Alex' presence, too, and he was telling me to greet this person and talk to him.

As the figure in the red coat grew clearer in my mind, I realized that it was me, as a boy of 17. Though I was certain of this, I asked him to identify himself. "I am the boy who came back from the dead," he said. "Don't you remember?"

He reminded me that when I was fifteen or sixteen years old I had contracted rabbit fever from a sick animal I had killed for the dinner table, and that I had been in a coma for nearly two days as a result. I had stood at that proverbial junction between life and death, fully aware that the decision to live or die was completely up to me at that moment. I remember this experience very clearly, even to this day. There was no fear. Death seemed to pose no threat. And I could not understand how to make the decision between life and death. Whichever choice I made seemed arbitrary.

That night I hovered somewhere above my body, from a distance of fifty feet or more. My body lay in the bed, packed in ice, in an effort to bring my fever down. I watched as my father entered the hospital room and dragged a chair up beside my bed. He was crying and holding my flaccid hand. I could not figure out why he was crying. I knew that my own death was near but I could not, for the life of me, understand the reason for his grief. Now that I saw death clearly I saw nothing to fear and nothing to grieve.

I had never seen my father cry like this. It mystified me that there could be such a powerful link between my dying and his grief. And I now believe that it was my curiosity about this mysterious link, as well as deference to my father's tears, that caused me to choose life over death at that moment. Had he not come to sit with my body at that moment I am quite certain I would have chosen death.

So I had come back from the dead. The struggle back was not easy. I returned to a body that was emaciated and weak. The fever had burned away virtually every hair and I found that I was blind, able to see only vague outlines of light and shadow. Indeed, I had been able to see more when my spirit hovered above the bed, free of my disease-riddled body.

Now, twenty plus years later, I was recalling all of this. Alex, my spirit guide, was making certain that I saw it, that I recognized that I was here, in part, to serve my father as he had served me. Except that this time I was to help him choose death and cross over. But there I was, sitting under a pyramid of cedar saplings, lashed together nearly two decades before, contemplating a dream figure in a red hunting jacket.

I asked the Boy Who Came Back From The Dead what he would do to help me. He said he didn't know, but that he would stay with me and when the time came that he could help he would let me know.

The next day when I went back to visit my father at the hospital he was worse. Much of the time he lay very still, his eyes closed. When he did awaken for a second or two he seemed not to connect with anything going on in the room. He frequently called me by another name and when he did I answered him as though I was that person. If he asked me to take care of something that wasn't there I obeyed.

Most of the time I sat by his bed and meditated, as before, with one hand on his chest. The image of the invisible vehicle carrying the two of us out over the desert was always there now but the ride seemed slow and sane and I did not grow frightened.

Toward evening I became aware of my older brother coming into the room and just standing there, staring at my father. I was deep in meditation, and was concentrating on the image of the vehicle, hoping it wouldn't speed up and frighten me. I was clearly aware of the fact that the speed of the vehicle was gradually picking up and there was nothing I could do about it.

The vehicle's speed increased by the second, so I finally asked for help from my inner guide. Alex appeared, simply looked at me, and then shrugged. He did not know what to do except to advise me to ask for help from The Boy Who Came Back From The Dead. Instantly, The Boy Who Came Back From The Dead appeared, saying that he could take my place in the vehicle now. He did this, and I watched as my father and he raced off. At that moment I felt relieved of a great burden, and I felt grounded and at peace.

Early the next morning my father died. He went in the most peaceful way imaginable, drifting off to sleep, never to awaken. But not before my older brother and I hugged him, told him that we loved him, and said goodbye.

Months after Dad died, my older brother described what had been going through his mind that evening when he entered the hospital room and stood so still, staring at Dad and me. My brother told me that he saw what appeared to be an ethereal copy of Dad's body floating above the bed, connected to the navel of the physical body below it by a thin, organic-looking thread. Nearly a year later my brother discovered, quite by chance, that yogins report that this is a common experience of people who are close to a dying person, and that it represented the spirit leaving the physical body.

Throughout those days of my father's dying, and even for weeks afterward, Alex continued to serve me. He maintained a calm presence, even during some of the most horrible and disconcerting, for me, moments. With his calm presence, he was always a touch stone for me, a reminder that my fear and trembling were of my own making, that seen from the higher perspective that Alex knew, my fears were no more than vanity.

Where Is The Proof?

There is no way to objectively confirm these experiences. The only part that can be confirmed is that my inner guides, Alex and The Boy Who Came Back From The Dead, clearly served important functions that allowed me to be with my father in ways that were helpful to him, to me, and hopefully to the entire family. Had I not allowed myself to receive the help I got from these inner guides, the entire experience could have been repulsive and fearful. With their help we were able to be with Dad, to give him our love and our caring even through the last moments of his life.

Mystic Sources or Imagination?

We know from our anthropological studies of ancient peoples, and from our study of the practice of "channeling," that when a person takes on the character of an animal, a goddess or god, or another person, they gain access to information that they don't have in their everyday lives. This practice is as old as story telling and the use of masks. Certainly, in the wearing of masks, something almost magical occurs. We change character. If we're willing, we *become* the character depicted by the mask.

There is a story told to me by a friend who lived for several years on the Zuni reservation, in New Mexico, where she was a gradeschool teacher. A single parent, she also brought up her own child there. One day, when my friend's daughter was seven years old, she was sitting on a wall watching the Katchina dancers as they paraded through town during Shalako, a traditional day of ceremony.

The Katchinas, the Zuni believe, are spirits who were once in human form. In their passage to the spirit world, they have evolved into higher beings who now return to Earth from time to time, to teach people certain spiritual principles.

During ceremonies, appointed people in the community don the masks of these spirits and through practice and ceremony they slowly assume the specific character of the Katchina. In many cases, the right to carry and act out a Katchina has been passed down in the same family, through many generations. This is considered a great priviledge and is taken very seriously.

My friend's child, sitting on the wall, was watching these traditional dances when her Zuni friend, of about the same age, turned to her and whispered, "Do you know the secret of the Katchinas?" My friend's daughter replied, no, she did not. The Zuni girl then whispered in her ear, "There's real people in there!"

Here was a child who probably knew each of the people dancing the Katchinas. Next door neighbors, cousins, the man who worked behind the counter in the local convenience store...all of them were people she'd be familiar with in the tiny village of Zuni. But so thoroughly did they assume the characters of the Katchinas that there was nothing to betray their everyday identity. The fact is, whatever the mask and costume represented to the dancer, had the power to allow the dancer to dissolve his own ego and personality self and adopt the mannerisms and the wisdom of the spirit figure. Indeed, this practice is a transcendent experience for most of the dancers.

In workshops where people access their own spirit guides, there are always many surprises. We have seen people assume the character of, say, an eagle, and describe the experience of flight. We've seen young people become grandmothers or grandfathers, speaking like them, even looking like them, and bringing closure to family mysteries or grievances. In one case, a woman who'd been quite reticent during a four-day workshop took on the character of a very entertaining and wise crone. Dancing about in a halting, yet graceful swirl of movement, the crone cackled like a raven, then stopped in front of each person in the room to give a bit of advice and insight totally appropriate for that individual.

These are all examples of working with spirit guides. Either outwardly or within the quietude of your own consciousness, characters appear who clearly access information, as well as a way of being, that you were not aware that you knew. This can, of course, be explained in several different ways. Perhaps by dropping some of our ego boundaries, or assuming different ones, we are activiting parts of our minds that we don't ordinarily access. Maybe the mind stores far more information than the everyday self is able or willing to allow into full consciousness. Somehow, by assuming different characters we switch channels and so become aware of areas of consciousness that were hidden away until then.

We know that when we write or read novels, we enter the lives and the minds of people very unlike ourselves. And we learn from this, our view of the world is changed, our perceptions broadened. For a little while we enter the lives of the characters we're reading about, or we share the thoughts and feelings of the author. The writer's skills create a container that holds us in worlds very unlike our own, and in the process we transcend our own limits.

If the spirit guide can be explained in these terms, as little more than products of the imagination, it does not, however, diminish the impact of this process on our lives. The ability to assume different characters for the sake of momentarily transcending your everyday perceptions of the world can indeed be valuable. This consciousness tool can enrich your life in quite extraordinary ways.

When he was a young man, C.G. Jung wrote a small book titled *The Seven Sermons to the Dead* (*Septem Sermones ad Mortuos*). In that booklet he reported on characters, or spirit guides, who instructed him in a way of looking at the world that was quite different from his scientific training as a physician and psychoanalyst. Indeed, to read this early writing the person who knows Jung's writing well will find the seeds for many of his most progressive and creative ideas that he developed during his extraordinarily productive life.

When we look at work such as this, and at other so-called "channeled" quality works of people such as Jane Roberts (*Seth Speaks*) or Helen Schucman (*A Course in Miracles*), and we compare the knowledge and experience of the *authors* to the knowledge and experience of their *spirit guides* we often find significant disparities. The dissimilarities, or even contradictions between the two suggest that the authors really are tapping into a source of information very different from their own. There is no way of proving this, of course, but after studying some of these *channeled* works, one is inclined to agree with Jung in his assessment of his own spirit guide, Philemon:

> Philemon and other figures of my fantasies brought home to me the crucial insight that there are things in the psyche which I do not produce, but which produce themselves and have their own life. Philemon represented a force which was not myself.

In his discussion of the role Philemon played in his

intellectual and spiritual life, Jung said that his spirit guide "represented superior insight...a mysterious figure to me. At times he seemed to me quite real, as if he were a living personality."

Jung also speaks of meeting a friend of Gandhi's, a spiritual leader from India, who Jung described as a gentleman of considerable sophistication and education. At one point, Jung asked the man about his spiritual education and what guru he had studied with. The man replied, matter-of-factly, that it was Shankaracharya. Jung, who knew this teacher as a commentator on the Vedas, who had died centuries before, was astonished. When he asked for clarification, the man replied that his guru was indeed the same person.

"Then you are referring to a spirit?" was Jung's next question.

The man replied that this was so and that there are many people who have spirits for teachers. For Jung, this was welcome confirmation for his own experiences with his early *Seven Sermons* as well as his later work with Philemon and other spirits.

In making use of his communications with spirit guides, Jung was actually working within a well-established tradition. For example, it is generally accepted that the Vedas, part of one of the oldest religious scriptures in the world, were based on revelations channeled by ancient Indian sages. In a similar way, according to Moslem faith, the Koran was channeled by Mohammed during long visionary states. In more modern times, the works of Alice Bailey were channeled to her by a spirit guide she identified only as "The Tibetan." Others we might add to this list include Pat Rodegast's *Emmanuel's Books,* and David Spangler's *New Age Transformations: Revelations,* to name but a few.

In Gnostic thought, as well as in many Eastern religions and the spiritual teachings of several Native American peoples, the universe and everything we observe, is of one consciousness. Further, we are not at all separate from this consciousness but a part of it. In his *Seven Sermons,* Jung's spirit guide calls this consciousness the "pleroma," and says, "We are the pleroma itself, for we are a part of the eternal and infinite."

As the *pleroma* itself, each and every one of us is capable of accessing anything that the pleroma embraces--which is everything. My own opinion is that were we to constantly be open to this infinite knowledge and infinite experience, we would probably go mad. To make it possible for us to function in our physical form, our brains, and in particular our personalities, or egos, act as filters, allowing us to keep our knowledge somewhat manageable. But when we access spirit guides, or even if we *create* them, we change those filters that our personalities provide. These different characters allow us to expand our own capacities and our own awareness, dipping into areas of the pleroma, with its infinite knowledge, that would otherwise never be accessible to us. I am reminded of the words of William James, one of the fathers of modern psychological research:

Most people live...in a very restricted circle of their potential being. They *make use* of a very small portion of their possible consciousness, and of their *soul's resources* in general, much like a man who, out of his whole bodily organism, should get into a habit of using and moving only his little finger.

Through work with spirit guides, we begin to move into the intuitive and mystical realm, an area of human experience that we have gravely neglected in our zeal to measure, categorize and quantify the universe. Perhaps through our explorations of the intuitive realm, blending modern techniques with ones that are thousands of years old, we can become more familiar with our "soul's resources" and how they can enhance the quality of our lives.~

Spirit Guides

Lifelong Spirit Companions

*This level of consciousness, like a
gigantic telephone exchange, affords
access to all other realms of awareness.*
—Holger Kalweit

Throughout our history we humans have sought ways to understand the *invisible forces* that govern our lives. By this I mean spiritual and emotional forces--the *soul's resources*--whose presence we know not by what our five senses tell us but by what our hearts and souls tell us. We know them through feelings such as love and compassion; we know them when we gaze at the heavens at night, observing the order of the planets; we know them when we hold a newborn in our arms and contemplate the mystery of life itself. In early societies, humans donned masks and costumes that personified these forces--the goddess of love, the fertility goddess, the god of war, etc.--to acknowledge and honor them.

As the actor or dancer dressed up in costumes and masks, and followed the rhythms of drummers, musicians and other dancers, he or she was transformed, seemingly abandoning everyday ego concerns to the divine character of the god, goddess or spiritual force they were depicting. The actors suspended their personal concerns and focused their attention on universal truths which we all know intuitively, though we may or may not ever learn to articulate them. The mask, costume, rhythms and movements all around them focused the actors' attention on the force or character they represented, giving them permission to transcend the physical boundaries of their own lives and focus more intently, through their hearts and souls, so that they might express truths beyond verbal understanding.

In my twenties and early thirties, I worked in the theater, fascinated by the way people with acting skills, and with the help of a good script, could access qualities and understandings they did not appear to otherwise have. The person who was meek and withdrawn offstage could become a convincing despot when he assumed a tyrannical character on stage. The woman whose life was a complete mess offstage became a noble leader on stage. I am convinced these transformations didn't happen only because the actor was being given the right words to say, or the dramatic setting to become a certain character. Surely that was part of it. More than this,

actors appeared to go through a personal trans-
formation. For that brief moment on the stage, he or
she embodied strengths and virtues that inspired or
horrified their audience, tapping into resources that
at times seemed nothing short of miraculous.

Knowing dozens of actors, on and off the stage, I
found it absolutely fascinating to ponder the puzzle
of how far the human consciousness was able to
stretch, how far beyond our everyday capacities we
can reach under certain circumstances. Indeed, there
were performances which absolutely convinced me
that consciousness itself has no boundaries, or at least
that it extends far beyond the confines of the bony
box that holds our brains.

Out of my experiences in the theater, I became
convinced that spirit guides start out as something
akin to characters in a play. Then, as we give
ourselves over to that character our individual
personalities slip away and our consciousnesses are
liberated, reaching into pools of awareness outside
our everyday self. By assuming these characters, we
create a way of experiencing a different reality.

In the summer of 1970, while visiting the home of
my doctor friend, Michael Samuels, with whom I
wrote several health books, we got into a discussion
about spirit guides. I expressed my theory that they
were something like sub-personalities that let us

look at life in a slightly different way, thus giving us access to a different perspective and possibly a vast new storehouse of knowledge. I fully expected Dr. Samuels to agree with me. Since he was a medical doctor with a scientific background, I believed he would take a skeptical, *scientific* position on spirit guides.

We were sitting on the deck at his Marin County home, enjoying a beautiful, clear day on the coast. In the distance, the ocean stretched out to the end of the earth, merging with a brilliant, blue sky. Down in Mike's apple orchard the trees were filled with fruit and a warm summer breeze carried their sweet fragrance. A hawk circled overhead. It was one of those idyllic days when there seemed to be all the time in the world to sit and talk.

Mike patiently listened to my theories about spirit guides. Then he said that a year ago he might have agreed with me, but since then he had several first hand experiences that made him ask some very different kinds of questions. Without arguing his case, he asked me if I had ever had an imaginary playmate as a child. I admitted I did indeed have one. In fact, I could remember him quite vividly.

Mike then told me that he had recently learned a way to get a "spirit guide," and asked if I wanted to give it a try. We talked about it for awhile and he described what the process involved--mostly going into a deeply relaxed place in my mind and becoming receptive to meeting a guide. It sounded simple enough, so I told him I'd like to do it.

Sitting in the warm sun that bathed the countryside, Mike instructed me to close my eyes as he talked me through what seemed like a simple relaxation exercise. As I relaxed, I let myself be guided my Mike's voice, asking me to imagine that I was standing in front of a house. The house that came to my mind was a very old one, built in the Tudor style, with its heavy, plank door opening out onto the narrow, cobblestone street. It was my impression that I was in a European city and that the house I was seeing was perhaps several hundred years old. There were cars around, so it wasn't as if I'd gone far back in time, but the makes and models were not ones I was familiar with, and most seemed to be from the thirties.

I had never been to Europe so it seemed odd to me that all this would appear so real, like visiting a place where I'd previously spent a good deal of time. I heard a bell ringing, far in the distance, tolling the time, and somehow knew it was coming from a clock tower in a public square not far away. I heard voices of passersby, and determined that they were speaking English, but with a thick British accent that I barely understood.

I commented on this to Mike and he told me not to talk but to stay focused on my imaginary journey. He told me to knock on the door of the house where I was standing. I did this. After a moment, I heard a lock being released inside. The door opened and a skinny young woman wearing a light green apron that covered the whole front of her body, greeted me. It was as if she had been expecting me. I did not know exactly what to say or do but this turned out to be unnecessary since she directed me up a wide staircase off to my right, and pointed to a door on the uppermost landing. I dutifully followed her instructions, assuming she knew more than I did.

At the assigned door, I knocked lightly. When nobody answered I went inside. It was empty except for a few straight-backed chairs, giving me the impression that this was a room which was never used. I reported what I saw to Mike and he suggested that I sit down in a chair and imagine seeing a door in front of me, through which my guide would come. The door was a special sliding door, opening at the bottom and slowly raising up so that I saw my spirit guide a little at a time. I sat down, as instructed. In a moment the door started opening, showing me the sturdy shoes of a woman with rather large legs. As the door inched upwards, I saw a white labcoat, a thick waist, and finally a complete person. Disappointed that it was not the imaginary playmate from my childhood--and quite surprised that it wasn't!--I nevertheless was curious and sat patiently, waiting to see what would happen next.

This new guide introduced herself to me as "Dr. Hilda." She was a middle-aged, somewhat overweight medical researcher with a Germanic accent and a very stuffy manner. She wore no makeup, her cheeks fleshy and plain, with jowls that made her face quite round. She had short, close-cropped, graying hair, and her starched, white, oversized lab coat made it impossible to get much of a sense of her body.

She was quite amiable, in spite of her stern appearance, and cordially offered to show me what she called her laboratory. I got up and followed her into a room with a lot of stainless steel and glass cases and tables. I asked Dr. Hilda what she was doing in my life, and she replied that she was here to teach me about some healing work she had been observing.

She told me to stand in a particular place in her laboratory, which I did. She took her place beside me and in an instant we were transported to an entirely different setting. We were now in a jungle, a dense, steaming atmosphere of very tall trees. I stood in a grove of ferns that towered over my head. Hilda put her finger to her lips, warning me to keep silent, then pointed to a clearing just beyond a border of green. I heard a man softly chanting, his voice deep

49

and resonant, the rhythms blending with the sounds of nature all around us. I asked Dr. Hilda what this was all about.

"It is a healing ritual," she said.

I peered into the clearing, careful to keep myself hidden behind the wall of ferns and broad-leafed plants. In the center of the clearing I saw two figures. The first was a very old and very wizened black man, sitting on the ground in a semi-lotus position, his head bowed and his eyes closed. He was naked except for something in his hair, which turned out to be leaves, or clumps of fresh herbs.

A second black man, this one younger and dressed in a white loincloth, danced around him. His movements were simple, rhythmic, and repetitive, barely varying as he circled the man on the ground again and again. He chanted as he moved, his voice deep, resonant, and soothing.

"What are they doing?" I asked Dr. Hilda.

"The man on the ground is dying, the other is a holy man, what you would call a medicine man. His name is Ubanga, or Uvani. Different people call him by different names. I believe one name is his common name, the other is what you call him when he is doing his work."

"Does he know you're studying him?"

"Yes, of course," Dr. Hilda said. "In this work, you do not observe without asking permission."

"And the holy man. What exactly is the medicine he is using?"

"Rhythm. His medicine is in the rhythms of his chanting and movements."

"Does it work?" I asked. I must admit that I was more than a little skeptical. I could not see how movement and rhythm could possibly heal anyone or why a medical researcher of Dr. Hilda's apparent status would think it a legitimate subject for serious research.

Dr. Hilda smiled. "Yes," she insisted. "Uvani is a great healer, and his dance is great medicine."

"What is the disease he is healing?"

"The fear of death. He is working with the man's resistance to death. Uvani is helping him make the passage. He knows the way because he has been there himself. In his youth he died after being bitten by a poisonous snake. But he came back from the land of death and now he helps others make this passage."

Let me note here that this occurred at least a year before my father's death and I believe was to be an important source of strength for me when I was called to his bedside. At the time of my introduction to Hilda and this bizarre jungle scene, I did not see how helping someone die could be called healing. To me, healing was outwitting death, not cooperating with it.

We stayed at the edge of the clearing for only a few moments, then Dr. Hilda said it was time to go back. Instantly, we were transported back to her sterile laboratory, with its white walls, stainless steel and spotless glass, a shocking contrast to the jungle setting where we'd watched Uvani.

Moments later, I shifted my focus again and was back on Dr. Samuel's deck, bathed in warm sunlight. As I opened my eyes and looked around, however, nothing seemed familar to me. This is difficult to describe. Although I knew exactly where I was, the world seemed fresh to me, as if I was seeing it for the first time. Coming from the imaginal world I'd just visited, and popping so suddenly back into my everyday life, I now felt as if everything around me was a fantasy. Reality had become story-book magic, where colors were too brilliant, and the depth of the landscape exaggerated, like viewing the first 3-D films with special glasses. Smells were intense, and I became particularly aware of the scent of the eucalytus trees and blossoming fruit trees all around the Samuels' property.

I continued to experiment with this spirit guide process, and in the fall of the following year I received another guide. This one came through in a dream. It is worth noting here that this is not at all unusual. You might, for instance, do the exercise for getting a guide and receive nothing at the time. But that night, or even several nights later a figure comes through in a dream, whose presence is so vivid and clear that you cannot ignore them. In any case, this is what happened for me.

This guide introduced himself to me as the spirit of a famous person who had been dead for nearly twenty years. He had been a writer, and I was somewhat familiar with his work. I knew him as a man who in real life had experimented with the occult. So it was natural that I would have gravitated toward his writing. Though I had never known him in real life, I admired him and felt I knew him, in many ways, as one might "know" a well-rendered character from a favorite novel.

I saw him as tall and slender, with thinning gray hair and piercing blue eyes so bright and lively they defy his age. He is more than a little clumsy in his movements, reminding me of a teenager who has not quite grown into his body. I usually picture him wearing a tweed sports jacket, a sports shirt open at the collar, and light tan dress pants. He always has a rumpled look about him, his outward appearance never having been high on his priority list, even during his physical life.

Not long after making contact with this entity, I learned that his widow was living in the United States, and with a little detective work on my part was able to contact her. Being curious to know if she had ever had any contact with him since his death, and wanting to see if I could corroborate some things about him, I sent her a book I had written, with a little note asking if I could either meet with her or talk with her on the phone. A month or two later, she called me and we spoke about her husband's interest in what she called "spiritism." She shared some stories about his experiences with spirit guides and we exchanged our own theories and beliefs about such phenomena. She admitted that she was not as much of a believer as her husband had been, had never experienced talking with spirits herself but said that she had always tried to keep an open mind about it. As the conversation drew to a close, she asked if I would be writing about these experiences, and I replied that I hadn't planned on it. But being a writer it was certainly a possibility. She then asked that if I did so, would I please not name her husband as my guide. I promised that I would keep his name a secret, a promise I've kept to this day. I said that if I did talk about him I would refer to him by the name of my childhood guide, Alex. For all I knew, the two might be merged spirits or total fantasies on my part. I liked the idea that maybe this new guide was a grown up version of the earlier one.

When I later told this guide of my conversation with his wife, and said that I was going to be calling him Alex from now on, he found all this quite amusing. He laughed and said that in spite of the fact that he did not picture himself as an Alex, it was quite all right if I called him that. After all, he said, in the spirit world there is very little need for names or any other of the trappings associated with the physical world. But as a person still embodied, I would not be satisfied unless I could picture my guides with names and physical bodies and clothing.

From the start, Alex helped me with my writing. When I wanted to get feedback about something I'd written, I had only to imagine him sitting across the desk from me and he would be there. He seemed to respect what I was doing, though he also seemed amused by it, in a nice way, I must add. He had clearly moved beyond the subjects which interested me but never gave even a hint of being critical or condescending. Alex was, and is, a gentle, kind entity, in spite of having an incredibly broad range of knowledge, on virtually every subject.

Within a few weeks of meeting Alex, I became quite accustomed to his presence, and stopped thinking of my association with him as anything unusual. I do remember, however, asking him to tell me about spirit guides. What are they? Do they really exist or do we fabricate them in our minds? Do they have autonomy, operating separate from, or outside, our own consciousnesses?

Alex said that spirit guides exist in our con-sciousnesses as the result of the same human faculty that allows us to dream. *But what, in fact, does it mean to dream?* he probed. He told me not to take dreaming for granted, that it was something very different than we assumed it to be in modern life. He said the easiest way to think about dreaming was to consider that our dream world--our sleeping dreams as well as the state we enter when working with spirit guides--is a parallel reality, existing side by side with consensus reality. It is not a "made-up" or "pretend" reality, but one that in fact determines the course of everyday reality. Were it not for this invisible reality, he said, there could be no physical reality. The invisible reality, he insisted, is our foundation.

Alex insisted that there exists an aspect of human consciousness that makes it possible to experience and understand things that are not available to us in the usual ways, such as reading, attending lectures, watching an informative television program, or living through a significant event. There are ways to access wisdom and experience things other than through our physical senses, or even our brains.

While all this was intriguing to me, I found myself looking for some objective evidence that all this had any relationship to my everyday life. I still could find no valid argument repudiating my original theory that channeling was primarily a creative process.

Then one afternoon, I became very sleepy. I crossed my arms, put my head down on my desk and slipped off into a restless somnolence. I was aware of Alex' presence, but this was not unusual since he was frequently there whenever I was writing. As I drifted off, I imagined myself transported to a rugged seaside setting. There was a high cliff at the edge of the ocean, and I was walking along a trail at the top. It was windy and cold and I shivered under a yellow slicker someone had given me for this walk. Far below me, the waves crashed over rocks, sending huge geysers of spray thirty and forty feet into the air. I believe it was the area around Big Sur, California, just south of Carmel.

"There are twenty principles in all," Alex was saying.

"Principles?" I asked, feeling disoriented, as if I'd just tuned in to the middle of a television program and had no idea what was going on. "What principles are you talking about?"

Alex ignored my questions and went on talking, lecturing me about these twenty principles. When I awoke, I remembered only little pieces of the dream--the walk along the spectacular coastline, the mention of the twenty principles, and my question about the number. Frankly, I was quite curious. The number "twenty" somehow seemed important, even though Alex had acted as if it wasn't. But what were the principles he was talking about? My memory of them consisted mostly of impressions.

Over the next few days, I entered into a long series of dialogues with Alex. Again he described the twenty principles to me, this time not in a dream but in waking dialogues that I recorded in my journals. I took the role of the student sitting at the master's feet. At other times, he took me on inner journeys to demonstrate the principles, as if the telling itself was not enough.

Today, I can honestly say that the twenty

principles have become key guidelines in my own life. Whenever I turn to them, for help in my own life, I find them extremely helpful. Alex described these twenty principles as "universal guidelines" that exist for all people. They are, he said, as ancient as humanity itself, and will endure as long as the universe itself endures.

"Certain things," he told me, "become necessary when spirit, which is infinite, takes on a finite form, as it does when we are born into a physical body. Given brains, personalities and bodies, we appear to be separate and autonomous beings. In that form, we try to make sense of everything. We are limited, however, to making sense with our brains, forgetting what we truly are, forgetting that it is impossible to separate ourselves from the earth, from each other, from our friends or enemies, since all, everything, is nothing more than a thought."

"Whose thought?" I asked.

"Can't be answered," he replied, enigmatically.

"Can't be or you won't?"

"*Can't be!* Your mind, mistakenly believing itself to be a model of all Creation, imagines questions which quite simply don't exist, and certainly aren't relevent. And that's the crux of the whole problem."

"Which problem?" I asked.

Alex laughed. "I think we call it *the human condition.* The twenty principles I gave you become necessary only as rough guidelines for help with the human condition. But I warn you, they are not truths. They are only guidelines, necessitated by the peculiar circumstances you've come into by taking on this physical form. Truth always exists outside any of the faculties connected with that form, so this is the best we can do. Live these principles *as if* they were true, but never insist that they are. What you learn from them will either serve you well or not at all. Use them only as long as they serve."

(For the record, I used the twenty principles Alex dictated to me in a book titled *Mind Jogger,* which is published by Celestial Arts. It is available through any bookstore, though they might have to order it. Or you can mail order it from us.)

I tell this story to illustrate some of the ways we can work with our guides and learn from them. But more than this, I'd like to make it clear that there are guides with whom we might maintain life-long relationships. It has been that way with Alex. I like to believe that the same spirit guide I have today is somehow linked with the much younger spirit guide from my childhood. I have asked but Alex' answers are more enigmatic than definitive. There's the implication that it is one of those questions that my brain likes to make up, but which is really of no relevance. What I can say for certain is that there appears to be a continuity between the earlier guide and Alex. He knows what went before and having that continuity with him is important to me.

I consider Alex a teacher and counselor and his presence in my life--whether imagined or real--is a source of both comfort and edification. He is, in a very real way, a bridge to that invisible reality to which all of us are bound. And he is a friend, one who knows my life well--perhaps better than I know it!

As I approach the end of this chapter I am reminded of a quote by Holger Kalweit, from his remarkable book on shamanism, *Dreamtime and Inner Space* (Shambala Publications, 1988). In that book, he describes the experiences of a person who has entered and returned from that invisible reality that we've come to know, at least a little bit, through our spirit guides:

"One person who returned said: 'It seemed that all of a sudden, all knowledge--of all that had started from the very beginning, that would go on without end--that for a second I knew all the secrets of the ages, all the meaning of the universe, the stars, the moon--everything.'"

Based on my own experiences with spirit guides, I have become convinced of at least two things: first, that there is a reality beyond that which we perceive through our five senses; and, second, that spirit guides can provide us with glimpses into the reality beyond our physical one, which like a nagging child demands so much of our attention. By establishing a practice of consulting with your guide(s) on a daily basis, this process becomes increasingly useful. And out of it comes a broader understanding of the invisible reality--that which is the basis of all life.

Going Forward

In the following chapter, you'll find instructions for getting a personal spirit guide. Read these over before you actually sit down to do them. Then go forward, knowing that literally thousands of people have used these instructions successfully, opening their hearts and their minds to a wonderful source of information and assistance.

If you are presently working with a psychotherapist or psychologist, I recommend that you talk over the spirit guide exercise with her or him before you do it. Share this book with them. If they feel that this inner work might interfere with your psychotherapy work, consider that possibility carefully before going on.~

Spirit Guides

Meeting Your Spirit Guide

The most beautiful thing we can experience is the
mysterious. It is the source of all true art and science.
                                        —Albert Einstein

I n entering this territory associated with the use
of spirit guides, it is natural to do so with a
certain degree of caution, or even apprehension. Our
apprehension grows from a realization that we are
moving into the unknown. And our caution comes
from recognizing that we are pioneering uncharted
terrain. To enter any new territory is to risk changes
in our outer life as well as our inner one. People who
have not had much experience working with the
inner world, or the world we associate with
transcendental or transpersonal realms, will undoubtedly find their world views challenged.

The human mind, however, is very self-protective.
When it detects that we are "getting in over our

heads," it always puts out warning signals, in the form of fear, doubt, and that little voice within that says, "This is stupid, a farce. Why am I bothering with stuff that common, everyday reason tells me is sheer nonsense!"

It is important to pay attention to these signals. Ask what's behind them. For example, maybe these warnings are telling you that diving into this realm is going to challenge important relationships in your life. Is there a loved one who fears what you are doing, or who finds such beliefs distasteful? Are there important religious, or even scientific beliefs that you hold that would be challenged if you discovered that this other reality was valid and useful?

If you wish to go forward with your exploration of spirit guides, first try to answer some of these basic questions: What's behind your resistance or fear? What would you have to change in your relationships, or in your own professional beliefs, or in your world view? Don't take these questions too lightly. Give them the respect they deserve but also recognize that you have options other than simply responding to the fear or resistance by backing away from the experience entirely.

The options are to question what your resistance, doubts and fears are about and then make a conscious decision about whether to go forward or not.

The novelist Andre Gide once said, "Don't understand me too quickly." This is always good advice where messages from our self-protective mechanisms are concerned. And it is the only way to move beyond our own prejudices, arrogance and superstitions.

The exercise you'll find here for meeting your spirit guide begins with deep relaxation. In a deeply relaxed state your mind slows and the visual cortex of your brain becomes more receptive and active. It is here, in the visual cortex, that the action of the spirit guide will first take place.

Much has been made, in recent years, of the importance of deep relaxation for exercises such as this. It is the kind of relaxation exercise that leads to the meditative state. In the meditative state, our brainwaves are altered; we grow relaxed, so relaxed that we let go of the tensions and worries of the day and soon our minds go blank, or nearly blank. In this state, we enjoy the feeling of having nothing to think about or act upon. For a moment we truly cut ourselves off from the cares of the world.

This deeply relaxed state is easily achieved with the following exercise, though it may take repeated practice (from three to six or more tries) before you feel you can achieve the deep state of relaxation at will.

For Newcomers Only

If you have never done a deep relaxation or meditation exercise before, the scenario will probably go something like this: You'll scan the written exercise, which will seem simple enough, almost too simple to be taken seriously. Then you'll decide to give it a try.

As you begin to relax, something comes to mind that you feel simply must get done before you go on. Or, you begin going over events of the day in your mind. Or you begin to worry about something that at that moment you can't possibly do anything about anyway. And everything that comes to mind really is important.

Let yourself fully acknowledge the thoughts and feelings running through your mind. But tell yourself firmly, *I do not have to act on any of these issues right now. It is perfectly all right to take ten or fifteen minutes for relaxing.*

The issues, like spoiled children, may continue to try to compete for your attention. Here's what to do if that happens:

Stop and make a conscious decision. Ask yourself, *should I stop relaxing, get up and do what I feel I must do, or should I let it go?* If you really feel you need to take care of something, do it. You can come back to relax when you are done. Your decision to stop your meditation and do something else is as important to the process of learning deep relaxation as is a fifteen minute session with no interruptions.

Final Tips On Doing This Exercise

For best results you may wish to do this exercise with a friend, having them read it to you as you follow the directions to relax. You might also wish to make a cassette tape of it on your recorder and play it back to yourself. If you do this, read the exercise into the recorder in a monotone. Read slowly enough so that you can complete each step of the exercise before going onto the next one. It may take some trial and error before you get the right speed and pacing for the tape, but keep at it until you can sit back, play the tape, and go into a deeply meditative state by listening to your own voice.

The alternative is to record your voice as you read the exercise to a friend. Watch your friend's responses as you read, slowing down or speeding up when you encounter obstacles or your friend has a difficult time following you or letting their body do the exercise. An effective tape of this exercise will be paced to match the rate at which you are able to respond to at a deep, muscular level to each of the instructions.

Some people prefer to just read the exercise a few times so that they can sit back, relax and simply recall each step, thus moving easily through the instructions at their own pace.

Choose whichever process works best for you.

Part One: The Relaxation Exercise

Make a conscious decision to take five or ten minutes to relax. Give yourself permission to use your time in this way. Choose a time of day and a place to work where you will be free of distractions.

~Sit in an alert, upright position, your hands laying gently, palms open, on the tops of your legs.

~Let your shoulders be loose and relaxed.

~Relax your toes and let the entire soles of your feet make contact with the floor.

~Loosen any tight-fitting clothing.

~Open your mouth and yawn, or pretend you are yawning.

~Let the areas around your eyes be relaxed. Let your forehead be loose. Let the area around your nose and mouth be relaxed.

~If ideas or feelings urge you to think or act at this time, pretend they are a ringing telephone in another room. You may observe the sound of the "ringing," but don't feel that you must answer. Simply focus your attention on the quality of the bell's sound and remind yourself that truly important thoughts or feelings will return, if you wish them to, after you have finished relaxing.

~Take a deep breath. Hold it for a moment. Slowly exhale through your nose.

~Be aware of your chest relaxing.

~Take a deep breath. Hold it for a moment. Slowly exhale through your nose.

~Be aware of your shoulders relaxing.

~Take a deep breath. Hold it for a moment. Slowly exhale through your nose.

~Be aware of your abdomen relaxing.

~Take a deep breath. Hold it for a moment. Slowly exhale through your nose.

~Be aware of your back and buttocks relaxing.

~Take a deep breath. Hold it for a moment. Slowly exhale through your nose.

~Be aware of your legs relaxing.

~Take a deep breath. Hold it for a moment. Slowly exhale through your nose. Feel the bottom of your feet where they make contact with the floor.

~Be aware of your feet relaxing.

~Now allow your breathing to return to normal. Enjoy this relaxed state.

~Just allow yourself to be in this relaxed state for a moment before you go on.

Part Two: The Exercise
For Meeting Your Guide

While in a deeply relaxed state, do the following to meet your inner guide:

Imagine that you are out for a walk.

You may be walking in a city. Or in a small village. Or in a woods. Or alongside a stream. Or near a lake or other large body of water. You may be in the mountains or by the ocean.

You feel safe. You feel confident. You are physically comfortable and at ease.

For a moment, just enjoy your walk.

You now approach a structure: it may be a small house, a large building, a rustic structure, a modern one. Stop for a moment and simply look at this structure.

Notice its size and style. Notice the area around it--other houses, open fields, etc.

You now go up to the structure. You are standing at its entrance. You knock on the door or in some other way announce your presence.

You hear a voice in your mind, or you get some sort of signal to enter and go inside. You do this, feeling confident, safe and comfortable.

Step inside. Close the door behind you.

Look around you. Take note of what you see: the color of the walls and floors, whether the rooms are bright or dark, the furnishings you see, any knick-knacks that come to your attention.

Somewhere in this house you will meet your guide. This meeting may occur in the room where you are now standing. It may occur somewhere else. You will know exactly where you should be for this meeting. Go to that place now.

Imagine that you are now sitting down in the room where the meeting will take place. You are facing a special door. It is a sliding door that will open from the bottom up.

Your guide is now standing behind the door, waiting to meet you.

The door slides up a foot or so, then stops.

You see your guides feet. Take your time, now. Note what the guide is wearing: shoes and socks? what colors and styles? Or is your guide barefoot?

The door slides open a little more until you are able to see everything up to their waist. Note what they are wearing. You may also see their hands at this time, if they are standing with their hands at their sides. Note any jewelry they might be wearing.

The door now slides up as far as their neck. Again, note their clothes, if any, their posture, their size. Note any unusual personal items--a scarf, necktie or kerchief, necklace, broach, items in their pockets, etc.

Now the door fully opens and you see your guide's face for the first time. Take as close a look as you like. Look at their hair. Look at their forehead. Look at their eyes. Look at their mouth and chin. Look at their ears. Look at their neck.

If is time to greet your guide. In your mind, or out loud if you wish, say "Hello, my name is _____. I understand that you are my inner guide. I'd like to know your name."

Your guide steps forward now and greets you. You may have a sense of them shaking your hand, or hugging you, or kissing you.

If you do not get a response right away, wait until you do get a response. This may come as a voice, clear and distinct like someone talking in the room where you are sitting, or it may come as a name that suddenly pops into your mind.

Imagine, now, that you and your inner guide sit

down together and begin conversing. Talk on any subject, but in the first meeting limit yourself to a few minutes exchange.

When you feel like stopping, simply tell your inner guide that you wish to do so. Tell them that you are glad you met them and that you will come back to be with them, and converse with them another time. Shake hands, or in some other way bring a cordial closure to the meeting.

Now leave the room where you met and go to the front door of the building. Go outside.

When you are ready, take a deep breath. Open your eyes if they were closed. Yawn. Stretch. Slowly get up and walk around.

After You Have Met Your Inner Guide

After meeting your inner guide, give some thought to the meeting. Did it go as you wished? Did this guide seem to be someone you would like to meet and talk with in the future? If not, recognize at this point that you need not see them again. You can go back at a later date, do the exercise again, and get another guide.

If you are not certain you want to keep your

guide, give yourself some time to think about it. There is no rush. And always remember, where your inner world is concerned you are the master. You may find things that surprise you but you can take control any time you wish.

If you didn't get an inner guide your first time around, don't worry. You can try again. Or, your guide may appear quite unexpectedly to you in the next day or two. The guide may even appear in a dream.

C.G.Jung reports that his first efforts to make contact with his inner guides were not without misgivings. At the time of his first experiments there was scant literature available on the subject of getting guides and working with them. He did not know if he could enter his inner world without "becoming a prey of the fantasies," and only after many years of exploring this inner world--both his own and his patients'--was he convinced that it was a safe territory to enter. The following describes his first experience of entering that world:

It was during Advent of the year 1913--December 12, to be exact--that I resolved upon the decisive step. I was sitting at my desk once more, thinking over my fears. Then I let myself drop. Suddenly it was as though the ground literally gave way beneath my feet, and I plunged down into dark depths. I could not fend off a feeling of panic. But then, abruptly, at not too great a depth, I landed on my feet in a soft, sticky mass. I felt great relief, although I was in complete darkness. After a while my eyes grew accustomed to the gloom, which was rather like a deep twilight. Before me was the entrance to a dark cave, in which stood a dwarf with a leathery skin, as if he were mummified.

Over the years, Jung entered this territory time and time again, and for nearly a decade explored and got to know the various figures he met there. He reports that he learned much from his journeys, especially from the inner guide he would call Philemon.

Most of the time people are happy with the guides they get. Let's assume that you will be, too. In the days ahead, take every chance you can find to think about your guide, just as you might do after meeting a new friend. In the process of doing this their presence may become quite vivid for you. I don't mean that you will see them appear in the chair across the table or beside you as you stand in line at the supermarket. But you may feel their presence in much the way you do when thinking about a close friend. Take advantage of this moment to share any thoughts you might be having with your guide. You needn't talk aloud to them. Doing it in your mind is just fine.

Conversations with your guide need not always be on serious issues. You may pass the time of day with them. You may even share stories or jokes. It is not at all unusual to build up trust in your guide slowly, making smalltalk, getting to know them one step at a time, before entrusting this new relationship with a problem that is important to you.

Are Inner Guides Infallible?

Like people with physical bodies, the spirit guides can provide knowledge, comfort, counsel--in short, nearly all the qualitites that we seek in our everyday human relations. And just as in other relationships the guides can be the source of conflict, frustration, and anger.

The same things are true of spirit guides as are true of the people in our outer worlds. The illusions they are capable of weaving are no different than the illusions we weave for ourselves, or which we allow those we love to weave with us. We must see the spirit guides as being just as fallible as other humans in our lives.

Regardless of what they might tell you to the contrary, always remember that your spirit guides are, after all, only human.

In workshops on getting spirit guides, there is sometimes a person who is worried that by doing this exercise they open up to the possibility of evil coming in. In answer to that, I believe that we all have spirit guides who are guiding us every moment of our lives. And it has been my experience that this exercise changes this in only one way: We become more aware of these guides. I have never seen a situation where people received guides that were not consistant with their own character and their way of looking at the world.

If anything, the ability to contact our inner guides should give us more, not less control of their influence in our lives. Perhaps we do get in touch with influences that are destructive, that scare us or make us unhappy in some area of our lives. If we do, this gives us an opportunity to cathart that influence or transform it into an asset. If we open a dialogue with a guide knowing that we always have access to our own best judgment, we clearly reserve the power to tell any guide we don't like, or don't trust, to just "butt out" of our lives. If you ever do feel that you are having difficulty getting rid of a guide you don't want in your life, look for a professional helper, such as a spiritual counselor, a shamanic healer or perhaps a psychotherapist who has had positive experiences with spirit guides in her or his life.

Sharing Your Experiences

Whenever you are considering sharing your insights, and the source of these insights, with another person, do so advisedly. Remember that we are living at a time in history when anything that cannot be validated scientifically, or perceived through the five senses, is viewed with great suspicion. Before sharing your information, or telling another person about your source, take some time to query them about their own beliefs. Above all, don't open yourself up to ridicule by confiding in people whose beliefs are so narrow or prejudiced that they cannot be at least tentatively open to what you've experienced.

A close friend of mine recently told me a story about his earliest experiences with his spirit guides. He first became aware of them when he was five or six years old, and was tremendously happy to have them in his life. However, when he tried to talk with his parents about the "voices" he heard, they were at first indulgent and then increasingly concerned. At last, when my friend was seven or eight, his parents began to talk about taking him to a psychotherapist.

Even at this young age, my friend knew that his guides were a positive influence in his life. When his parents finally did take him to a therapist, the boy told the psychologist that he knew they were "make believe" but they sometimes helped him think things through when he felt confused. The therapist saw my friend two or three more times, then told his parents that what the boy was doing was harmless, and possibly quite healthy.

After that, my friend's parents not only tolerated my friend's spirit guides, they spoke of them more openly and supportively. This was tremendously empowering for my friend, who uses spirit guides in his work as a psychotherapist, focusing specifically on the issues of creative people.

Big Brother

When I was a child, my most helpful guide was a big brother figure who I have called Alex. However, in this day and age, "big brother" has other connotations. A few times in workshops, people have raised the question, "If I get a spirit guide, won't it be as if he is always watching me and judging me? Will I cease to have any personal privacy?"

While I have never known a person who got a "Big Brother" sort of guide, I have known one person who fantasized that his grandmother was watching and judging him. However, he also admitted that he had been raised by his grandmother who was "a strict and bitter old woman with extremely Puritanistic ways." His experiences with his spirit guide allowed him to see what a strong influence she continued to be in his life. And he also saw that she was not a spirit guide at all but a memory from the past. He was grateful that his work with spirit guides brought this emotional fact to light for him, because it did allow him to liberate himself from old programming.

Always keep in mind that we have a great deal of choice about our guides, and we have tremendous control of them. We can choose to respond to them or not, regardless of how adamant they may seem to be. In the final analysis, it is you who will decide that what they have to say is valid.

The bottom line is this: Spiritual work has a single goal--to make the world a little better, to improve how we relate to each other and the world around us. If you are faced with a choice that could result in you or any other person being harmed, always choose to do no harm.

Overnight Sensations & Other Illusions

I remember a young man in a workshop we taught in Northern California many years ago who decided at the last minute not to go through the training because he was certain that if he did get a spirit guide it would launch him into instant fame. He was just sure that this would happen. But even moreso, he was certain he was not yet "mature enough" to handle his imminent fame. In spite of our assurances that the chances of this happening were a billion to one, he nevertheless left the workshop and, to my knowledge, never got a spirit guide--and never became famous!

While this may seem like a joke, perhaps it is not so funny after all. Many people fear becoming more visible in their lives. It is a fear that we experience whenever we get nervous about speaking to a large group of people. It is, after all, much easier to live anonymously, to be alone with our fantasies, our dreams and our fears. To expose ourselves to others, whether one person or a million, is to be launched into a way of being that is very unlike the quieter, less visible life. As an anonymous person we never have to really struggle with that point of contact when we put our own fantasies, dreams and fears to the test in the "real" world.

So perhaps the young man who feared being launched into fame by his guides has a lesson for all of us; maybe some of the reluctance we have to seek our spirit guides, or maybe reach into the best in ourselves in other areas, has to do with our fear of fame. It's a subject worth raising, though its solutions are clearly beyond the scope of this book.

Another aspect of the fame issue has to do with

the person who is seeking a guide because he or she is convinced it will make him "special" and/or famous. Invariably, what happens in this case, is that the person's anticipation of all this happening becomes like an opposing magnet pushing away any guides who might *enter.* Sadly, the person does the exercise over and over, never to meet with any success.

My belief is that our first encounter with spirit guides is not unlike our first experiences with sex. If we go into it with the idea that it is going to be "life-altering," chances are we're going to be disappointed. Or worse, we may never be able to even open that door where we discover how spirit guides (or sex) will, indeed, alter our lives. These experiences do in fact alter our lives but the changes we experience occur over time. Often we don't recognize how life-altering they really are until, in retrospect, we look back over the years and are able to review how our lives unfolded after that initiating event.

At the very least, go into the study and use of spirit guides with a *beginner's mind,* that is, with as few preconceptions as possible. And also with an open mind about how they are going to serve you. The best, most creative and positive guides you'll get are not ones who are going to be slaves to your ego needs, which of course includes issues around fame, fortune and domination over other forces or individuals.

Working with spirit guides requires that we be open to the real mysteries of life. Through them we often gain knowledge that we cannot learn from other teachers or books; in the mystical realm, to which our spirit guides belong, knowledge comes through only when we let go of what we *think we know or understand* and allow ourselves the luxury of basking in the light of the *unknowable*. If this sounds like a contradiction, you're absolutely right. It is! But such contradictions lead us to truths that lie beyond anything we can validate or reason through with the inherent limitations of the human mind itself.

Mythology, Mysticism and Universal Wisdom

Joseph Campbell and Carl Jung both believed that we each hold within ourselves an inherent wisdom that is as old as the universe itself. Carried from generation to generation, as if by the genes, this wisdom nevertheless remains beyond our reach as long as we cling to modern man's faith in the scientific and technological methods of knowing. Campbell believed that one way to get in touch with wisdom that lies beyond the capacities of technology and science was through mythology. He believed it was not a coincidence, or a matter of repeating the same stories, that the same themes kept recurring in mythology. He believed that by studying the heroes and conflicts and sources of harmony expressed in mythology we could get in touch with the universal themes and issues of human life. He often stated that mythology was an "expression of the collective unconscious."

That term, *collective unconscious*, was one that Carl Jung introduced. It is the belief in an awareness that reaches far beyond individual experience or knowledge. It is the river of universal wisdom that touches us all. In his own life, Jung gained access to this wisdom through the use of spirit guides such as Philemon, and others. For Campbell, that wisdom came by studying the themes expressed in mythological characters.

We may or may not ever know exactly the nature of our spirit guides. Are they tricks of the mind, whereby universal themes and wisdom are embodied, that is, given a *persona*, human qualities that we can easily identify with--even have conversations with? Or are they, as Jung suggested, somehow separate from our personalities and our emotional or psychological needs? Certainly they do have very definite personalities, at least like the characters who Joseph Campbell discovered, appearing again and again in the rich mythology of people from every continent throughout the globe.

Do we need to answer who they are? My own conclusion is that we simply work with them. Put them to the test, if you will. Watch to see what happens as you follow their guidance. In my own life, this process has led me to my own joys, my own bliss, better and ultimately more reliably than any other process. Still, I do not know exactly what they are. Nor have I ever gotten to the point that I totally surrender to their guidance. I am still of the opinion that our own discernment is an important part of the lesson we are here to learn.

The growth and expansion of that discernment, past self-interest to an ever-greater harmony with the universal order, is perhaps our greatest challenge. Spirit guides may not have all the answers but they can certainly take us close to the core of that challenge and possibly give us the *second sight* we need to see beyond our own illusions of knowledge.~

About Tenacity Press

Tenacity Press is dedicated to the publication of books and tapes that expand our understanding of intuition, creativity and spiritual development. The press was established in 1991 and continues to make available materials that we hope can serve people who are seeking to make their own lives purposeful, joyous and meaningful.

While we do everything we can to produce high quality books that are easy to read and free of distractions such as typos and errors, we are, alas, only human. If you find errors or misinformation, we'd appreciate hearing from you so that we can have an opportunity to correct our mistakes. Write to us at the address you'll find below if you have comments. We will respond.

We regret that we do not accept outside manuscripts to be considered for publication. Our purpose is to have Tenacity Press stay small enough to be responsive to our readers. To do that, we know that we need to keep the operation simple, enjoyable and focused on subject matter rather than on what we can do to grow a big commercial success. Until we find a way to do both, we will cling to our modest publication goals.

Thank you for your support of our efforts!

Tenacity Press
Post Office Box 2710
Ukiah, CA 95482

ABOUT THE AUTHOR
AND HIS COLLABORATOR

Hal Zina Bennett, Ph.D. is the author of 25 books. He has spent his life studying, teaching and writing about personal growth, creativity, intuition and the wonders of the human consciousness. He and his wife, Susan J. Sparrow, teach workshops throughout the United States.

Susan J. Sparrow is a teacher, promotional consultant and writing coach. In addition to her work teaching and consulting, her passions in life include holistic health, gardening, and grandmothering. She is the co-author of *Follow Your Bliss* and series editor of *Emerging From Invisibility.*

~ ~ ~

For information about the authors'
workshops, books and tapes,
or to receive their free newsletter,
"*OPENING INWARD*," call Susan at:

1-800-738-6721